more ANTIQUE
QUILTING DESIGNS

ROBERTA BENVIN

American Quilter's Society

P. O. Box 3290 • Paducah, KY 42002-3290
www.AmericanQuilter.com

Located in Paducah, Kentucky, the American Quilter's Society (AQS) is dedicated to promoting the accomplishments of today's quilters. Through its publications and events, AQS strives to honor today's quilt-makers and their work and to inspire future creativity and innovation in quiltmaking.

EDITOR: HELEN SQUIRE
GRAPHIC DESIGN: LYNDA SMITH
COVER DESIGN: MICHAEL BUCKINGHAM
PHOTOGRAPHY: CHARLES LYNCH

Library of Congress Cataloging-in-Publication Data
Benvin, Roberta.
   More antique quilting designs / by Roberta Benvin.
      p. cm.

   Summary: "Quilting designs from pre-Civil War quilts. Includes patterns for Triple Irish Chain and Carolina Lily. These floral quilting patterns are suitable for classic or contemporary quiltmaking"--Provided by publisher.
   ISBN 1-57432-909-X
   1. Quilting--Patterns. 2. Patchwork--Patterns. 3. Flowers in art. I. Title.

TT835.B3556 2006
746.46'041--dc22

                    2006009537

Additional copies of this book may be ordered from the American Quilter's Society, PO Box 3290, Paducah, KY 42002-3290, or online at www.AQSquilt.com.

Proudly printed and bound in the United State of America

DEDICATION

To my grandbabies –
Hannah, Jonah, and Zaidyn

ACKNOWLEDGMENTS

To family and friends for their continued support.

To the generous quilt owners who invited me into their homes (or in some cases, allowed me to abscond with their quilts for a week or two) while I traced the quilting designs.

CONTENTS

Introduction 4–5

Sampler Designs
    CAROLINA LILY APPLIQUÉ QUILT, C. 1850 6
    TRIPLE IRISH CHAIN QUILT, C. 1850 16
    STAR OF BETHLEHEM QUILT, C. 1850 30

Variations on a Theme
    SUNFLOWER/COMPASS PIECED QUILT, C. 1857 . . 51
    TRIPLE IRISH CHAIN QUILT, C. 1860 68

Nook and Cranny Designs
    COXCOMB/TULIP VARIATION QUILT, C. 1868 84

Helpful Sizing Suggestions 94

About the Author 95

INTRODUCTION

I'm a firm believer in the adage that "the quilting makes the quilt." Every stitch breathes life into the fabric. Perhaps that is why I appreciate a quilt that has had as much emphasis given to the quilting process as to the construction and the choice of fabrics.

Contemporary quilters know that elaborate and extensive quilting is a necessity in order to achieve a ribbon or prize at today's quilt shows. Even though there are dozens of varieties of batting types to choose from–all of which require less quilting to hold the layers together–there is still an emphasis on the amount of quilting as an important element in competition. Whether old or new, a quilt covered with quilting stitches is enough to take your breath away. But I am especially in awe of an antique quilt with beautifully executed quilting designs, while imagining a quiltmaker who was, undoubtedly, merely finding an outlet for her creativity with relatively little reward or acclaim.

The quilting process has not always been considered as anything more than a functional step in a quilt's construction. Quilts in the late eighteenth and early nineteenth centuries had what we would consider very utilitarian stitching. The majority had only straight-line or, possibly, clamshell quilting. It was not until the era that has come to be known as the "Cult of Domesticity"–the period from approximately the 1830s through the 1850s–that all aspects of quilting and, indeed, all needlework in particular, reached the highest level of craftsmanship. This was the era of the Baltimore Album quilts; and it was also when we see spectacular quilting and the use of fanciful quilting designs. This is the time period that captures my attention the most, and on which I tend to focus my quilt searches.

In my first publication, *Antique Quilting Designs*, I chose quilts from the mid-1800s that illustrated the relationship between the quilting patterns and the influence of Pennsylvania German folk art. In this sequel, the quilts do not adhere to any particular theme other than their construction in the days before most patterns were commercially available. Their beauty evolved from the imaginations and creativity of women we know little or nothing about. I have tried to select quilts with wider-ranging origins, placing them in my own (strictly personal) system of categorization.

My intent is, once again, to provide today's quiltmakers–particularly those with an interest in reproducing antique quilts–with a selection of designs provided by nineteenth-century artists whose "canvas and brush" were a square of muslin and a needle.

SAMPLER DESIGNS

A wide variety of quilting patterns are used within the same quilt. Refer to pages 6–50 for three quilts that feature motifs that can be used together or as separate patterns.

VARIATIONS ON A THEME

Each of the patterns shown in these two quilts shares a basic design element, with block-to-block modifications. Refer to pages 51–83 for a bevy of beautiful patterns suitable for quilting, embroidery, and/or appliqué.

NOOK AND CRANNY DESIGNS

The quilt shown on page 84 showcases seemingly spontaneously-drawn designs that were drafted to fit a specific area. Patterns are on pages 85–93 and can be enlarged or reduced to fit any size area. See Helpful Sizing Suggestions on page 94.

CAROLINA LILY c. 1850

CAROLINA LILY QUILT

Origin: New York state. Maker: unknown.
Collection of Deborah F. Cooney.

Whenever I see a Weeping Willow on a quilt, experience has taught me that there is a good chance that it comes from either Boston or from New York state. Such is the case with this Carolina Lily quilt, which has a graceful willow design in the quilting.

Although, in the Victorian language of flowers and the sentiments that they represented, the Weeping Willow is generally considered a sign of mourning, there is nothing mournful about this delightful quilt. Perhaps there was another reason why this motif was a regional favorite.

CAROLINA LILY QUILT

CAROLINA LILY QUILT

Carolina Lily Quilt

CAROLINA LILY QUILT

TRIPLE IRISH CHAIN c. 1850

TRIPLE IRISH CHAIN
Origin: Chewsville, Maryland. Maker: Catherine Thomas.
Collection of H. Robert Leese.

I first "discovered" this quilt while it was on exhibit in the Hanover Area (PA) Historical Society. The Irish Chain pattern is used so frequently that it appears to have been a favorite choice of mid-nineteenth century quilters to display their repertoire of quilting designs. There is a look of elegance and sophistication in the six different designs that were drafted for the plain alternate blocks by a quilter with obvious artistic talents.

connect

connect

connect

connect

connect

connect

connect

connect

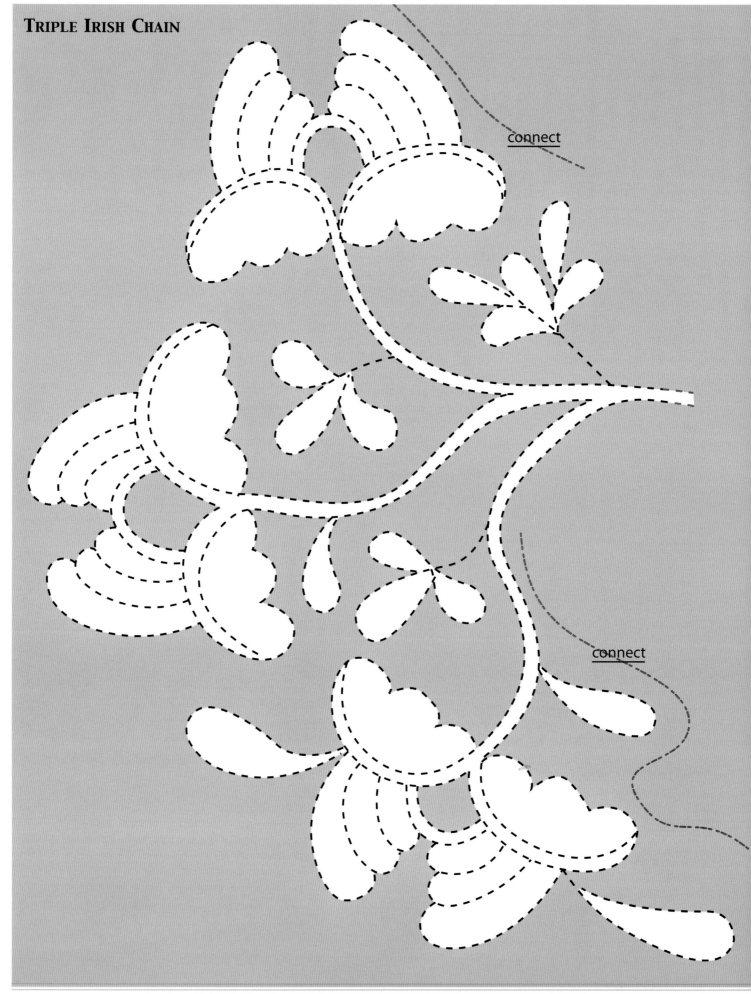

connect

connect

connect

connect

connect

connect

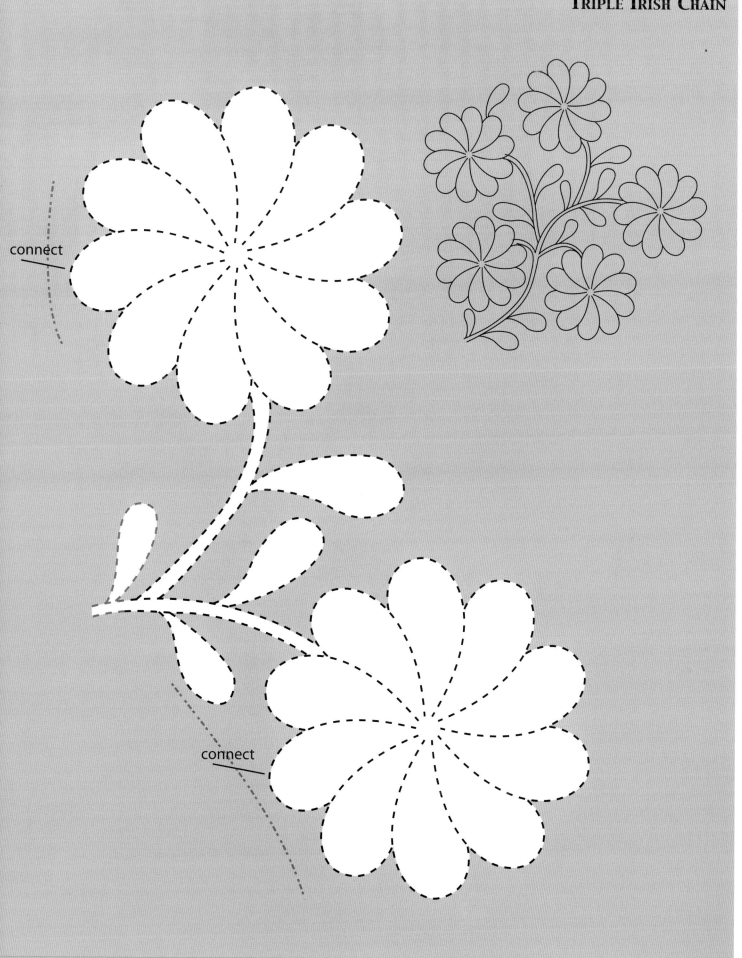

connect

connect

TRIPLE IRISH CHAIN

connect

connect

more ANTIQUE QUILTING DESIGNS *Roberta Benvin*

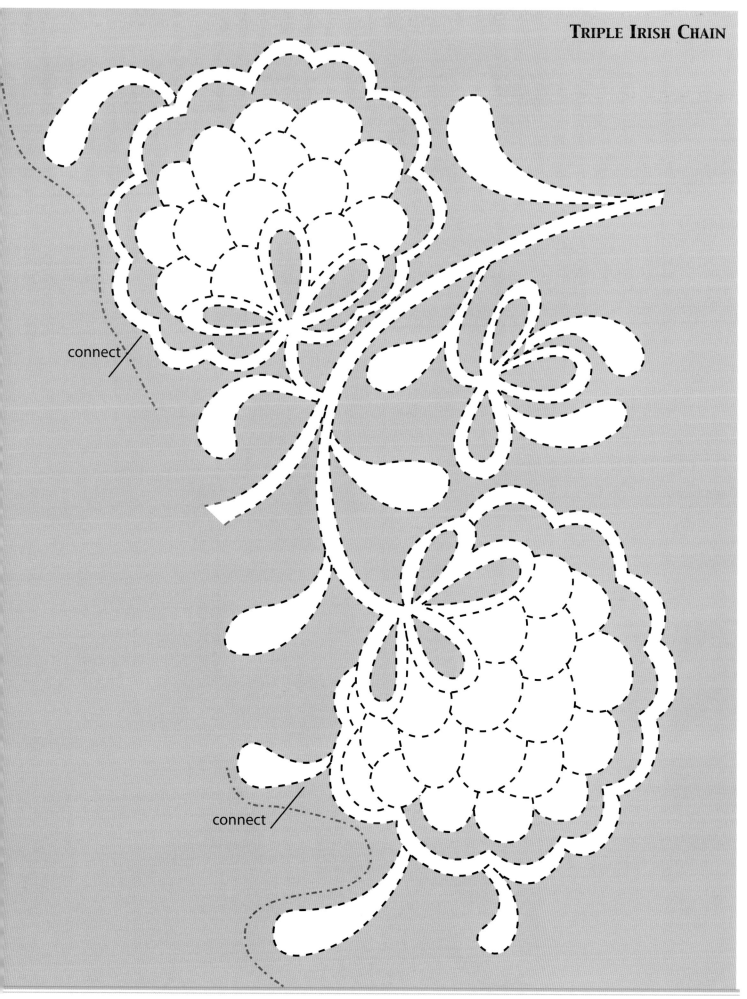

connect

connect

STAR OF BETHLEHEM c. 1850

STAR OF BETHLEHEM
Origin: York County, Pennsylvania.
Maker: unknown, probably Pennsylvania German.
Collection of James F. Adams.

The Pennsylvania German-made Star of Bethlehem typically has embellishments in the corner blocks and/or edge triangles. In this example, there are satellite stars in each corner and folk art-type quilting designs in the four large triangles.

As a tribute to the quiltmaker's imagination, each of the small squares and triangles in the satellite star blocks is different from one another. That is an assortment of thirty-two designs which can be used in numerous quilt patterns.

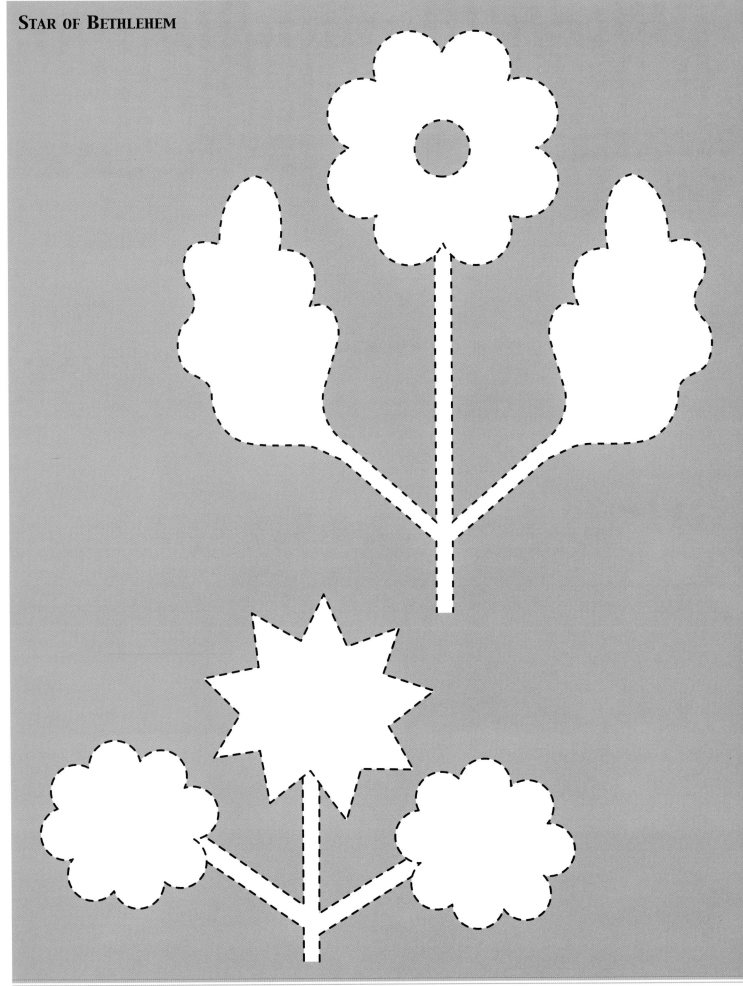

more ANTIQUE QUILTING DESIGNS

Roberta Benvin

Enlarge 150%
See page 94

Enlarge 150%
See page 94

Enlarge 150%
See page 94

Enlarge 150%
See page 94

SUNFLOWER/COMPASS

Origin: York County, Pennsylvania. Maker: Sarah Miller.
Private collection.

Could the quiltmaker have known this pattern by the name Compass Rose? Is that why each of the quilting designs is a variation of a rose, both realistic and stylized even to the extent of appearing exotic?

Sarah and her sister, Rebecca Miller, were both producing stunning quilts at the same time in their early twenties. Rebecca must have been the more flamboyant of the pair, because she proudly appliquéd an 1857 date and her initials in each of the four corners of a quilt she made in that same year.

more ANTIQUE QUILTING DESIGNS *Roberta Benvin*

more ANTIQUE QUILTING DESIGNS

Roberta Benvin

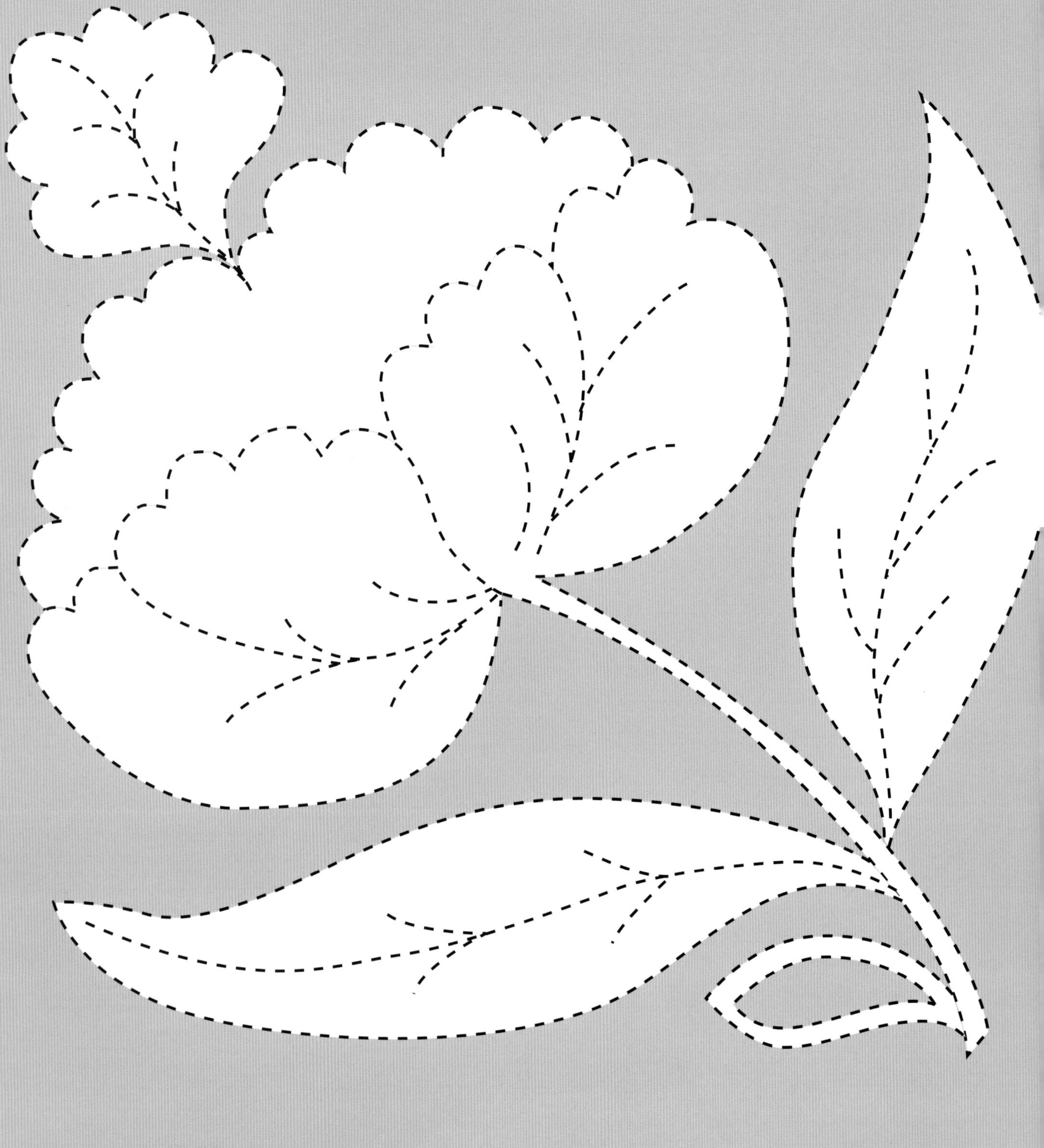

Sunflower/Compass

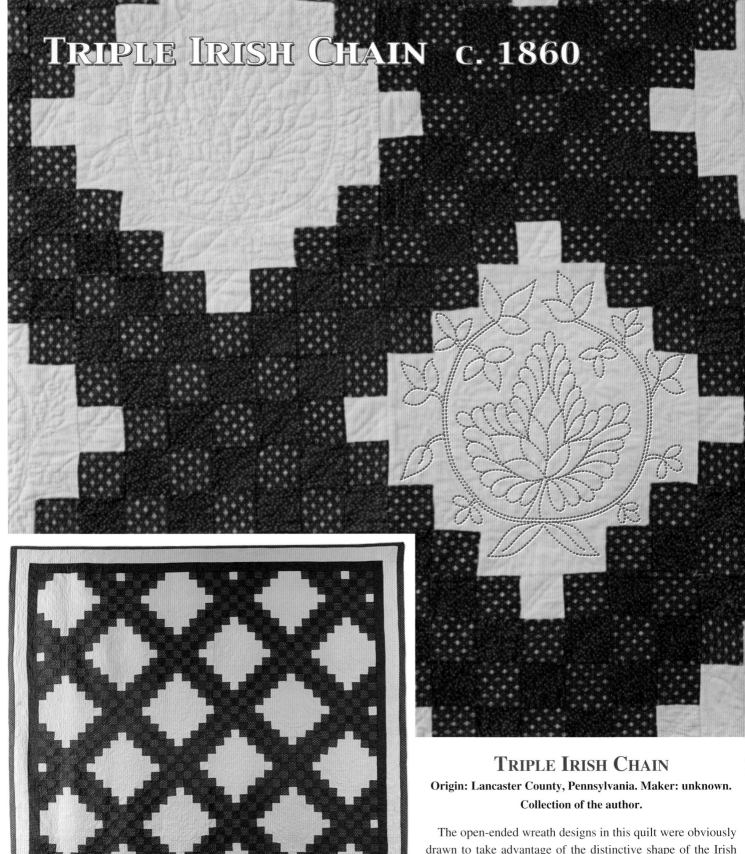

TRIPLE IRISH CHAIN c. 1860

TRIPLE IRISH CHAIN

Origin: Lancaster County, Pennsylvania. Maker: unknown.
Collection of the author.

The open-ended wreath designs in this quilt were obviously drawn to take advantage of the distinctive shape of the Irish Chain's alternate block. Additionally, in the second of the three borders, the quilter drafted a gently curving stem and lined it with motifs taken from each of the blocks; thereby, all of the elements were pulled together into a cohesive design.

TRIPLE IRISH CHAIN

connect

connect

connect

connect

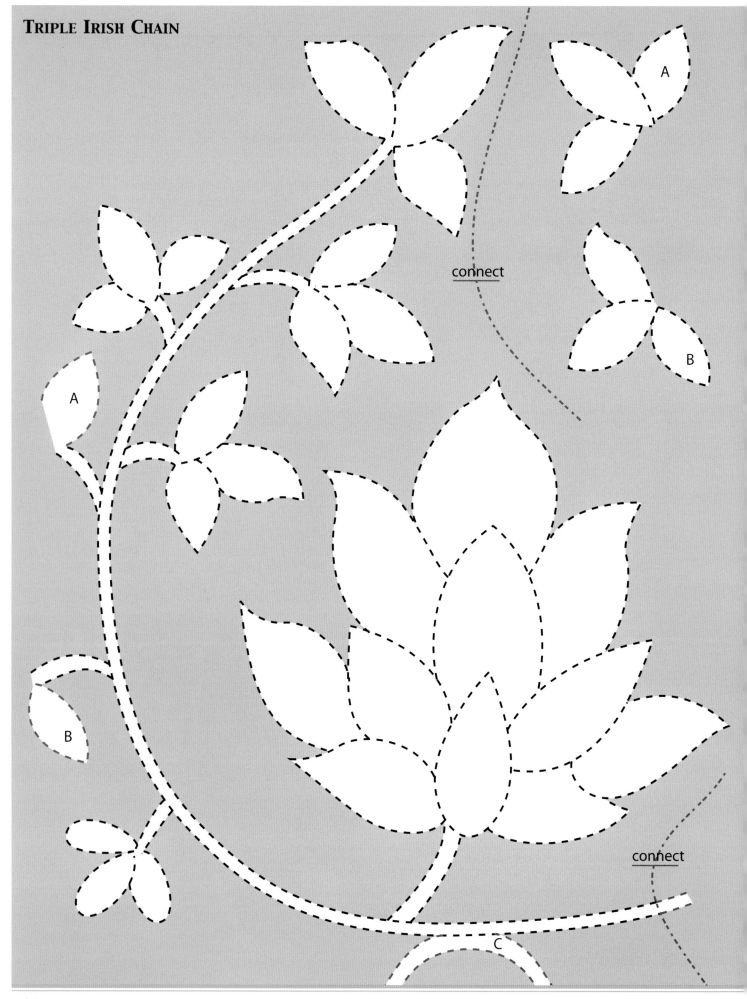

connect

A

B

A

B

connect

C

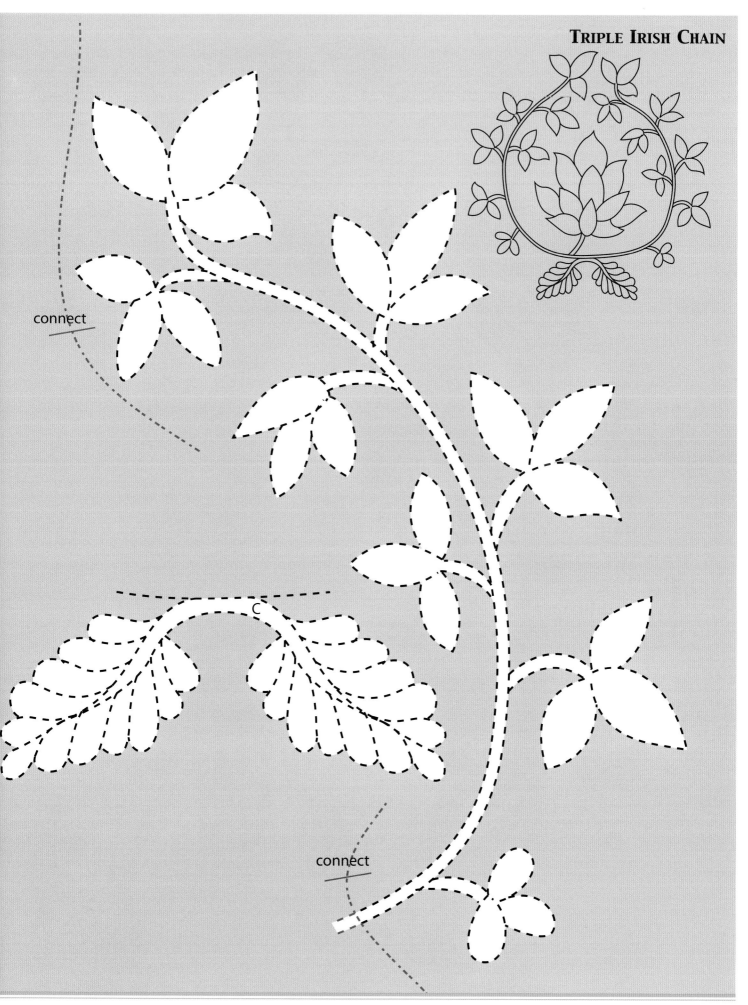

connect

connect

connect

connect

c

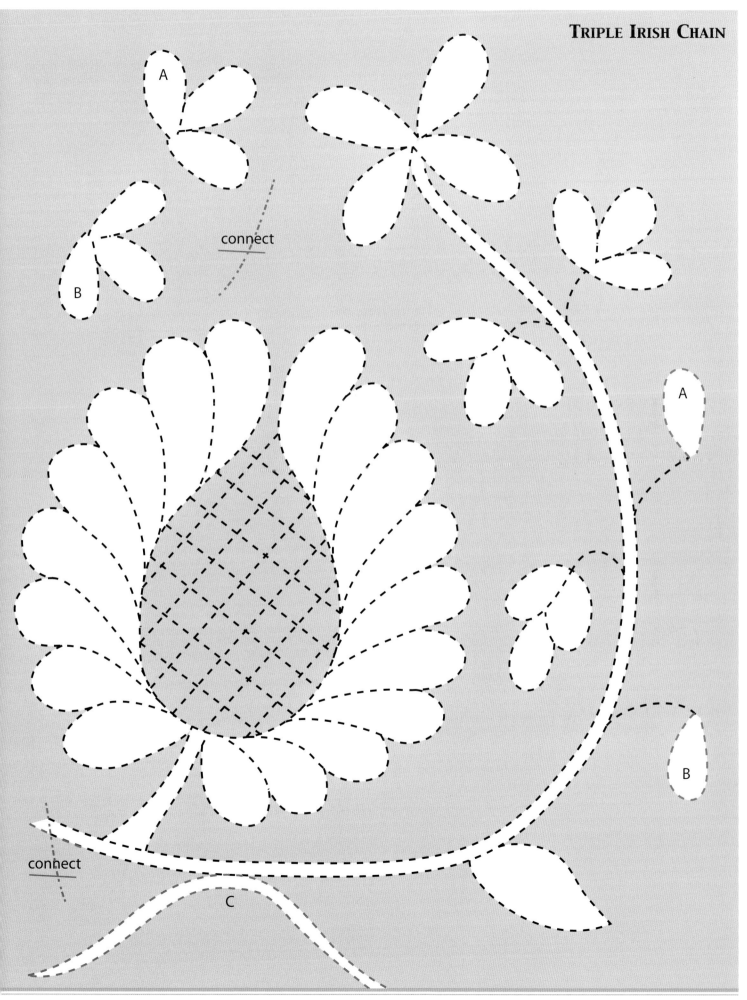

A

connect

B

A

B

connect

C

connect

A

B

C

connect

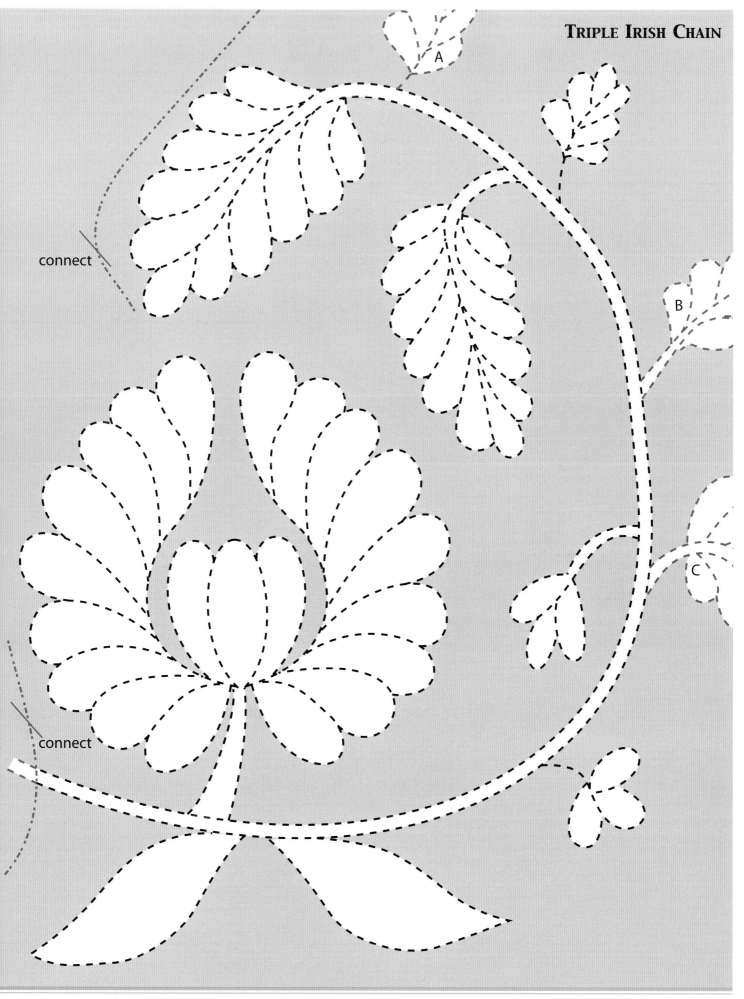

A

connect

B

C

connect

connect

TRIPLE IRISH CHAIN

A

connect

connect

more ANTIQUE QUILTING DESIGNS

Roberta Benvin

A

connect

connect

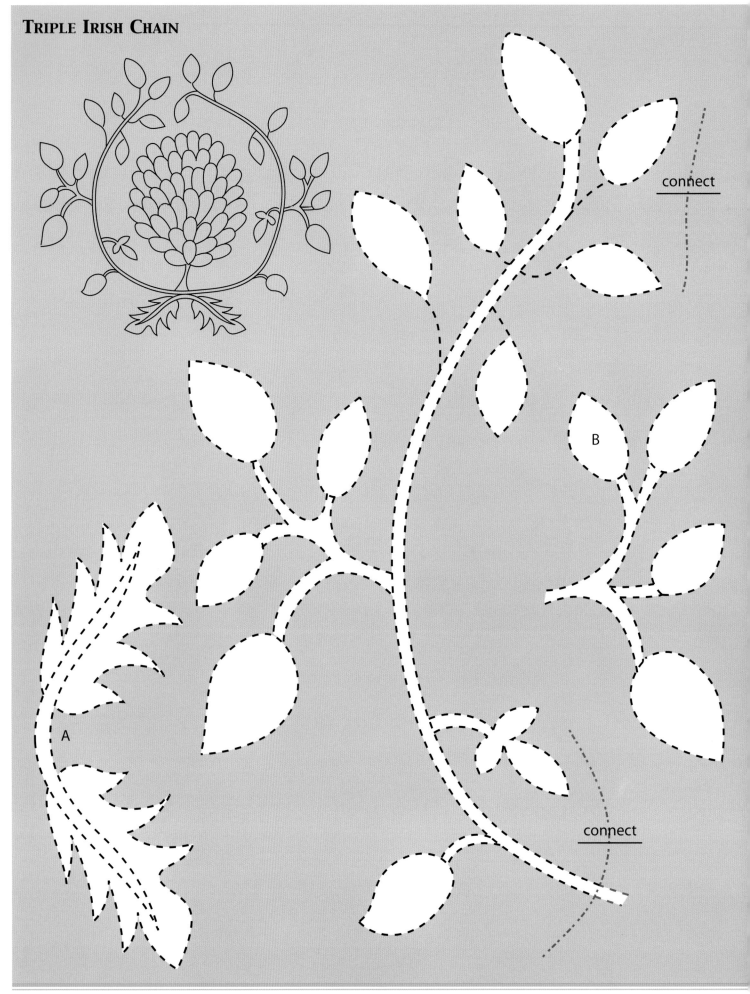

connect

B

A

connect

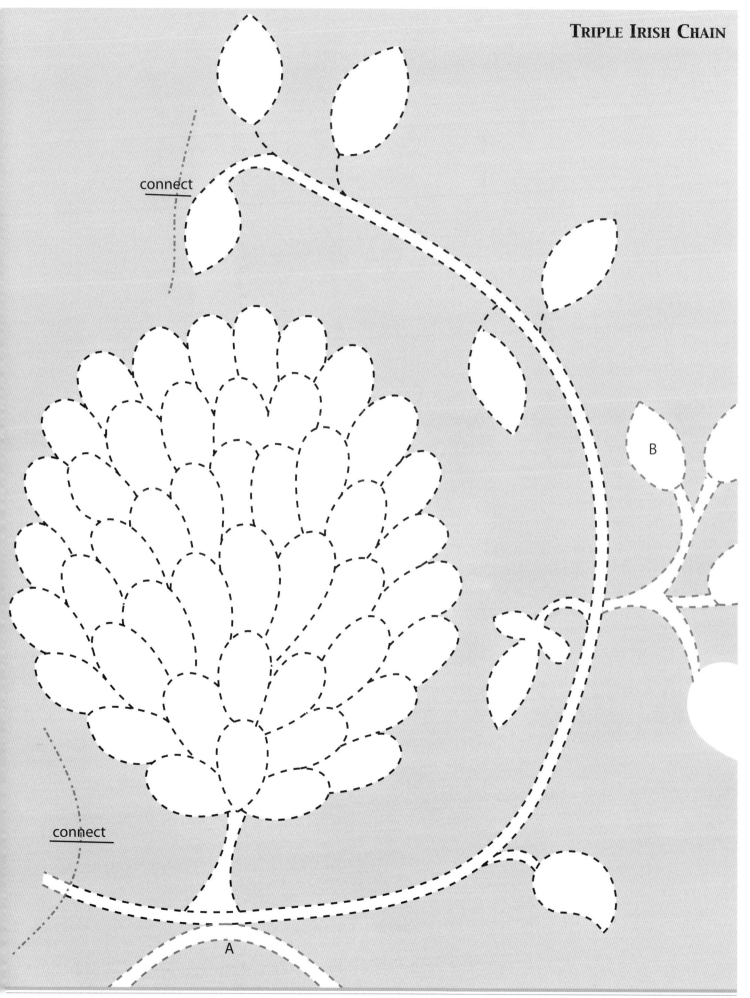

connect

connect

A

B

TRIPLE IRISH CHAIN

connect

connect

connect

connect

A

A

COXCOMB/TULIP VARIATION c. 1868

COXCOMB/TULIP VARIATION
Origin: possibly Ohio.
Maker: unknown–MS and 1868 inscribed in quilting.
Collection of the author.

The thin layer of cotton batting (the filler of choice for most early quiltmakers), which was sandwiched between the quilt top and backing, needed to be held in place with close stitching to prevent the cotton from shifting and pulling apart. When plain alternate blocks did not separate the pieced or appliquéd area, an overall pattern such as parallel lines usually covered the entire quilt. Once in a while, however, a quilter (such as "MS") would, instead, fill the spaces with a variety of spontaneously-drafted, original designs.

Coxcomb/Tulip Variation

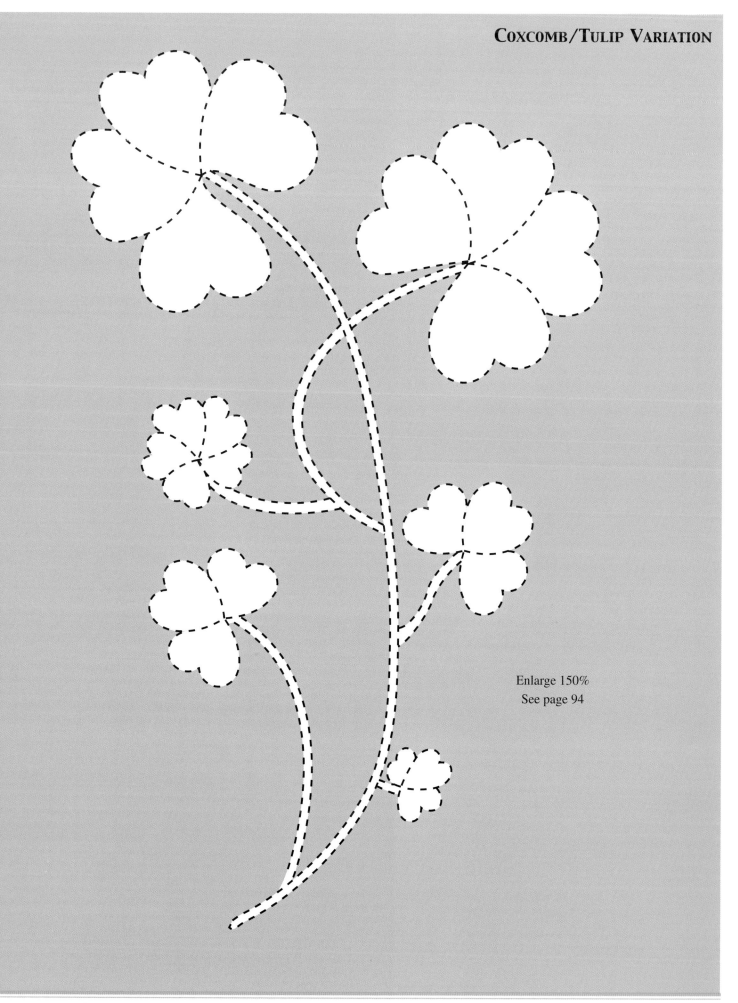

Enlarge 150%
See page 94

Coxcomb/Tulip Variation

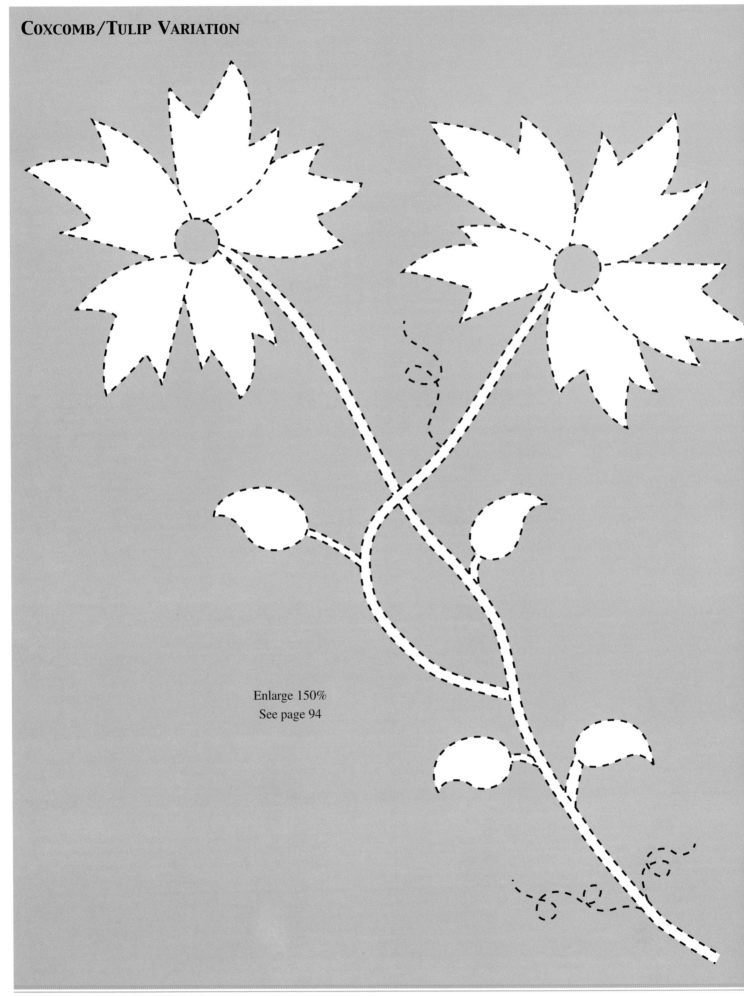

Enlarge 150%
See page 94

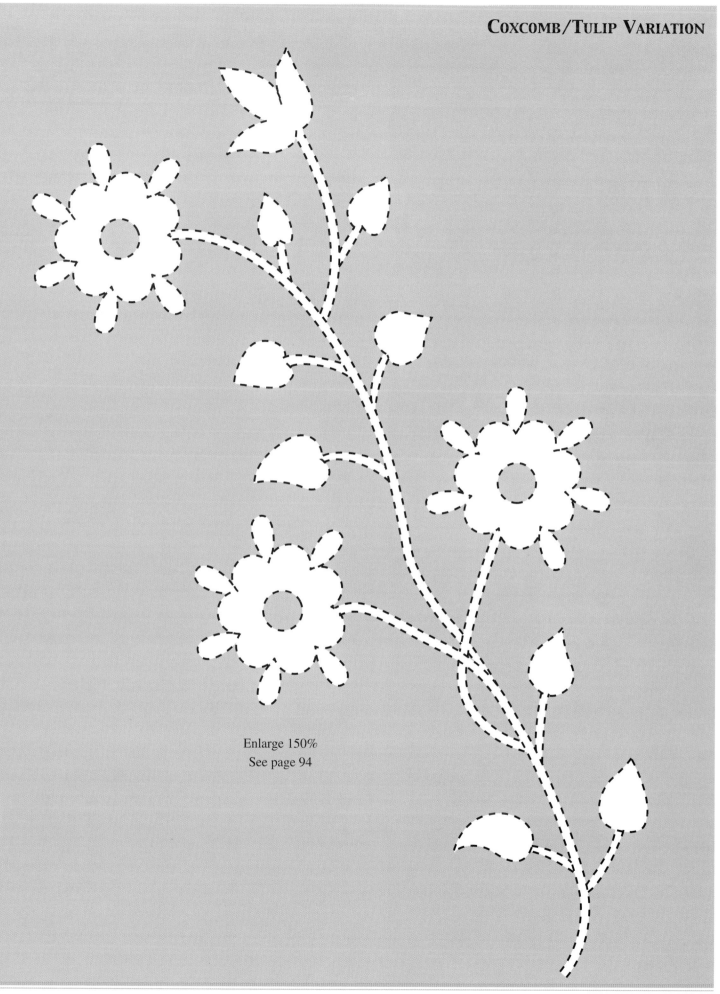

Enlarge 150%
See page 94

HELPFUL SIZING SUGGESTIONS

On the STAR OF BETHLEHEM quilt, page 30, the triangles between the star points are quite large. The patterns had to be reduced in size to fit the 8½" x 11" format of the book. You have my written permission to reduce or enlarge them to any size needed for your individual quilt project. A proportional wheel, sold at quilt shops and arts & crafts stores, can help you determine the proper percentages needed.

In COXCOMB/TULIP VARIATION, page 84, the patterns also were reduced to fit the page. The size of the flowers and stems were 13½" and redrawn to 9", a 67% reduction. They can be returned to their original dimensions by photocopying at 150%, as indicated on the pattern pages.

Remember: Photocopying pages can cause some distortion. This is not as critical a problem for quilting as it is with patchwork patterns, as the final size(s) for the quilting designs can be flexible.

The SUNFLOWER/COMPASS quilt, page 51, has sixteen beautiful floral designs featured on left and right facing pages. When photocopying, ask to have a photocopy made on clear acetate. For very little money, you will have an accurate transparency that allows you to reverse the direction facing both ways.

The original block sizes for the quilts in this book ranged between nine and twelve inches. If you would like to make the designs fit a block size of your own choosing, here is a chart that will help you take the pattern desired and either enlarge or reduce it to fit the new block size.

ENLARGING & REDUCING CHART

	6"	7"	8"	9"	10"	11"	12"
6"	100%	117%	133%	150%	167%	183%	200%
7"	86%	100%	114%	128%	143%	157%	171%
8"	75%	87%	100%	112%	125%	137%	150%
9"	66%	77%	88%	100%	111%	122%	133%
10"	60%	70%	80%	90%	100%	110%	120%
11"	54%	63%	72%	81%	90%	100%	109%
12"	50%	58%	67%	75%	83%	92%	100%

For block sizes not listed on this chart use this formula:

Desired block size ÷ Original block size x 100 = percentage

ABOUT THE AUTHOR

It seems a natural course of events that Roberta Benvin should combine her love of both history and quilting, and find her niche in the world of antique quilts. She is passionate about her quiltmaking, collecting, teaching and lecturing, and restoration work. Her documentation of antique quilting designs has resulted in this, her second book, and a line of quilting stencils manufactured and distributed by Quilting Creations International, Inc.

In 2003, she was asked by the Rotary Club of Paducah, to curate their antique quilt exhibit, held simultaneously each year with the American Quilter's Society quilt show.

In 2005, her first collection of circa 1845 reproduction fabric, entitled Antebellum, was released by P&B Textiles. Currently, she is working on a collection that features fabrics in quilts belonging to the York County (PA) Heritage Trust, made famous by the 2005 issue of McCall's *Vintage Quilts* magazine.

Several of her quilts, both antique and of her own design, have been featured in *Quiltmania*, a French quilting publication, including the cover quilt of the December 2005 issue.

Roberta is a graduate of Penn State University and operates her own dog grooming business.

OTHER AQS BOOKS & CDs

This is only a small selection of the books and CDs available from the American Quilter's Society. AQS books are known worldwide for timely topics, clear writing, beautiful color photos, and accurate illustrations and patterns. The following items are available from your local bookseller, quilt shop, or public library.

#6900   12" x 9"   us$24.95

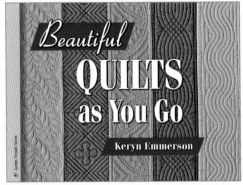

#6803   12" x 9"   us$22.95

#6678   12" x 9"   us$22.95

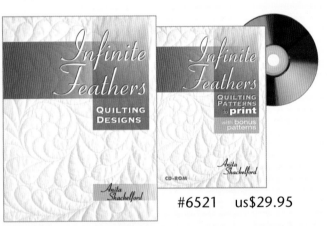

#6521   us$29.95

#6072   us$25.95

#6099   us$29.95

#6006   us$25.95

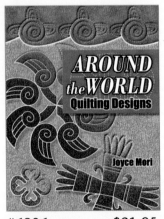

#6806   us$21.95

#6800   us$22.95

#6288   us$29.95

LOOK for these books nationally.
CALL or VISIT our Web site at

1-800-626-5420
www.AmericanQuilter.com